HEART SPEAKS

VERSES UNVEILED

SHREYA ANIL

Made with ❤ on the Notion Press Platform
www.notionpress.com

For Shivani , my lovely sissy who turned 10 months...

Contents

Foreword

***Heart Speaks* speaks about the innumerable thoughts lingering in unison like a flickering light of a candle that can diminish if not found a space on some nude pages of a virgin book. The book embraces the genre of poetry from where words jump out of the moist tongue to get printed on the pages and be one with the book.**

Preface

I happen to pen a few verses during the days of pandemic that outraged the modesty of the innocent cognitive mind that often led to me creating a few lines that my heart spoke to me. The journey of me writing these poems were moments of ecstasy that I had experienced while juggling with words and penning them down. I wish my readers too feel elated by reading what my heart spoke to us.

Acknowledgements

My wholehearted acknowlegement to Notionpress to publish my collection of poems Heart Speaks and to God almighty for being the child of my parents who always have supported throughout my journey of writing. My gratitude to all the readers who are holding my book in hand with much anxiety and love.

Prologue

A unique piece of work that's named Heart Speaks is a collection of poems that an adolescent girl writes giving wings to her fantasies and expressing the follies and foibles of her heart that feels, that breathes, that lives every moment thinking about what awaits next that has to be conquered. The collection of poems imbibe the happiness, the sorrow, the emotion unidentified that must deboard the words at the destination that leads to the heart of my readers.

1. The Last Period

White washed walls with
white- black boards
four ceiling fans
with lit no speed
twenty benches sitting here
fully tattooed.
We are the future carpenters
from nowhere but schools.
Carving on our benches
in between big lectures.
So many ears
listening to the blah
making sound with legs
fingers spinning pens.
Sitting fully bored
yet our faces acting interested
sitting for hours
waiting for break.
Oh ! it's so complicated
but its our obligation.
Lunch in our tummy
heads all sleepy.

Yes ! Its the last period.
Those cycles await,
the bell rings
and we are all at home.
These are the future memories
we'll be cherishing from home.

2. Chef -d'oeuvre

Beautiful beautiful its so beautiful
the aurora of nature
which we can't keep for later,
specially the apricity
makes it so haimish,
the beautiful trees
its the birds querencia
when the temperature is in fire
they give a lil zephyr.
I see many wayfarers
passing through the carrefour
this is so whimsical
that it got me lost day dreamimg
seeing the cosmogyral birds.
I feel like a solandis in solitude
What's this beauty
may be we call it
nature's chef- d'oeuvere.

3. Never Felt so Fake

When they blabbered things I didn't like
and started to decry
but I still decided
to fake a smile.
When their words were invective
and their actions all agregious
but I still decided
to pretend like I never defy.
I realized that I changed
for some disloyal dogs
coz that wasn't me
and I never felt so fake.

4. Coz My Way is Different

When the teacher starts her lecture
I pretend like I'm listening
I stare in her eyes
but it's just me daydreaming.
It's the time I feel
the most alive .
I get so lost
wandering in my thoughts.
I'll be Alice
but not in a wonderland
and I'm Tiana
but I kiss no frogs.
I'll be Rapunzel
and I'll cut my hair short
I'm Cinderella
with boots and not mops.
I'll be Red riding hood
but my hood is never red
I'm the Snowhite
but with no dwarfs.

I'll be Belle
but i got no beast
I'm the Lil' mermaid
but not under the sea.
I'm the Beauty
but I dont sleep
I'm Juliet
but i dont need a Romeo.
I'm not one in the herd
not one from the pack
I walk alone
coz my way is just different.

5. Soft Sea

Her mind was a sea
in which people threw stones
but never realized
how deep it goes.
She inflicted many emotions
like storms that hit hard
and shook the soft sea
left many scars
that remains forever
like a terrible eternal dream.

6. Empty Heart

When I wanted to talk
and share a lot
but there was no one
and i thought of writing it down.
It took me hours
to think what to write
but in the end
the paper was blank.
Coz the emptiness of the paper
could describe my heart
more than the words
from my head ever could.

7. Beautiful Lies

It has turned into a hobby
to gossip about everybody
talking behind people's back
which are not true facts.
Spitting so much trash
and making it all flash
people are agog
to get so much tea.
A group of morosis
the world have become
and we are waiting
for a meriorism !

8. Her

She was a kaleidogyn
with a sophrosyn
she had scars
but they made it her flaws.
Her skin wasn't fair
but she didn't care
she was insociant
but they made her a patient.
She had the neart
but they tore her apart
she was serafic
but they were terrific.
She is the creation of god
they were all wrong
they started to prate
and told it was her fate.
She had imperfections
they made her insecure.
All of them twattled
but she was in a battle.
She had cancer
It wasn't her fault.

The were demons
they mocked her so bad
without realizing
she was in a war.
She was so broken that
she wanted to whelve herself
They called her malefic
and made her nefarious
that she ran into the woods
thinking it was her fate
and got so tired that finally
she disappeared into the arsh.

9. Cycling on a Rainy Day

On a rainy evening
I'd go cycling
I could hear the storms roar
through the depressed clouds.
The sky is about to cry
and I'll smile
it throws raindrops on my eyelashes
and I'd look through to see
if the world is inverted.
Fallen flowers on road
yellow , white and more
even though dead
I'd not be cruel enough to kill it again.
So I'd go circus with my cycle
you'll see people running.
A last roar and it rains heavily
I'll rush to home
splashing all the mud
yet so happy to be drenched !

10. Beyond the Sea

Far beyond the sea
a ship you should see
in it lived a raconteur
for years and years.
He wrote so many stories
he had so many stories
countless number of stories
but no one to hear.
He was so dolorous
he had no one
the only thing he talked to
was a big old mirror.
The mirror is the one
who knows all his stories
he wrote so many stories
that he forgot to write his.
He didn't know the way
to get out of the sea
a big wave hit
and the mirror shattered.
His heart broke down
just like the mirror

now that the mirror is gone
he got so alone.
Guess it was his fate
to be an orate
and an old agelast
until his last !

About The Author

Shreya Anil is voracious reader and a girl in her 15 who finds solace in penning words that could speak the thoughts that lingers each and every moment in her mind. She started writing her first poem at the age of 10 and then the journey begins in accompaniment with words and verses as her better friends. The collection of poem Heart Speaks speaks her heart's desire to be with the solitary blank page and create a saga of being one with the book that speaks back to her.

Printed by Libri Plureos GmbH in Hamburg,
Germany